J

232.91 Butcher, Geoffrey
Bu
        Mary, the mother
        of Jesus

MARY
the mother of Jesus

© 1984 Rourke Publications, Inc.

Published by Geoffrey Butcher 1983

Published by Rourke Publications, Inc., P.O. Box 3328, Vero Beach, Florida 32964. Copyright © 1984 by Rourke Publications, Inc. All copyrights reserved. No part of this book may be reproduced in any form without written permission from the publisher. Printed in the United States of America.

Library of Congress Cataloging in Publication Data

Butcher, Geoffrey.
    Mary, the mother of Jesus.

    (A Little Shepherd Book)
    Summary: Simple text and illustrations retell the New Testament story of Mary and how she came to give birth of Jesus.
    1. Mary, Blessed Virgin, Saint—Juvenile literature. 2. Christian saints—Palestine—Biography—Juvenile literature.   3. Bible. N.T.—Biography—Juvenile literature.   [1. Mary, Blessed Virgin, Saint.   2. Bible stories—N.T.]   I. Title.   II. Series.
BT607.B83   1984   232.91   83-20191
ISBN 0-86625-242-8

MARY

the mother of Jesus

Written and illustrated by
GEOFFREY BUTCHER

Rourke Publications, Inc.
A Little Shepherd Book
Vero Beach, FL 32964

God sent an angel to Mary who was to be married to Joseph.

The angel told her that she would have a baby. He was to be called Jesus.

The angel also told Joseph to take Mary home as his wife.

One day the Emperor said that he wanted all his people counted.

Joseph took Mary to Bethlehem. They would be counted there with his family.

Many people were in Bethlehem. All the inns were full.

Joseph and Mary slept in a stable. It was there that Mary gave birth to Jesus.

They made a little bed
for the baby in a manger.

An angel appeared to shepherds in a field nearby.

He told them to go and find a
child in a manger. He would
be the Saviour.

They found Mary, Joseph and the baby in the stable. They worshipped Him.

Wise men also came from the east. They were looking for the new king.

They followed a star until it stopped over the stable.

When they saw Jesus and Mary they bowed down. They gave Him presents.

King Herod was angry when he heard of the birth of a new king.

The angel came again to
Joseph. He told Joseph to take
Mary and the baby to Egypt.

Herod told his soldiers to kill all the baby boys in Bethlehem.

Joseph, Mary and baby Jesus ran to Egypt.

Time passd. An angel told Joseph to take Mary and Jesus home to Nazareth. It was safe.

When He was twelve Jesus was taken to the Passover feast in Jerusalem.

On the way home Mary and Joseph saw that Jesus was not with them.

They ran back to Jerusalem to look for Him.

They found Him talking with the teachers in the Temple.

Everyone there was surprised.
Young Jesus was so wise.

Mary told Jesus they had been worried when He was lost.

Jesus said that He had to spend time in the house of God His Father.

They returned to Nazareth. There Jesus grew up in strength and wisdom.

Questions to help you understand

1. What did the angel tell Mary?
2. Why did Mary and Joseph go to Bethlehem?
3. How old was Jesus when He went to the Passover feast in Jerusalem?
4. Where did Mary and Joseph find Jesus after losing Him?